THE ULTIMATE

Key West

BAR GUIDE

MARK LEE

DUVAL STREET, "PARTY CENTRAL" IN THE HEART OF OLD TOWN KEY WEST.
PHOTO CREDIT: MARK LEE

CONTENTS

INTRODUCTION

Cayo Hueso, Key Weird, and Key Wonderful...these are all terms that have been used at one time or another for that tropical outpost at the end of A1A in the Florida Keys known as Key West. Once you leave the Florida mainland and enter the Keys, you find a group of islands that are in many ways more Caribbean than American. In fact, Key West still shows much of its Cuban and West Indies influences at every turn in its architecture as well as its food and drink. You may be surprised to learn that Key West is closer to Cuba than the mainland United States. Cuba can be found a mere 90 miles across the Florida Straits from the southernmost point down at the corner of South and Whitehead Streets.

Mild and warm in the winter and hot and wild in the summer, Key West is a tropical paradise where all sorts of pleasures can be found. Whether food or drink is what you seek, this town has much to offer as we will discuss later. Whether you are looking to do the Duval Crawl, hoist one with the locals over on Stock Island, or if you're just trying to find that lost shaker of salt, Key West is the perfect destination to do it all or nothing at all. Just kick back and relax on the beach and enjoy the view of the emerald-green waters and let the waves wash away the stress you may have brought with you to the islands.

Key West has been referred to as an amusement park for adults fueled with alcohol. Whether deserved or not, we'll let you decide. It has biker bars, wine bars, formal bars, clothing optional bars, Hemingway and Buffett bars, and, of course, the out-of-the-way locals' bars. Looking for a margarita, hurricane, beer, shooter, wine or that perfect martini, you'll not find more beautiful and inviting locales to explore. So hold on as we set sail for that tropical paradise and visit the bars of Key West.

Key West

THE BARS

Half Shell Raw Bar

231 Margaret Street
Key West, Florida 33040
305-294-7496
Monday thru Thursday 11:00 am – 10:00 pm
Friday thru Saturday 11:00 am – 11:00 pm
Sunday 12:00 pm – 10:00 pm
Happy Hour is daily 4:30 pm – 6:30 pm
www.halfshellrawbar.com

With a long and storied history as a destination on Key West's waterfront and most recently featured on the cover of Kenny Chesney's hit single, "When I See This Bar," the Half Shell Raw Bar embodies everything good about the laid-back lifestyle of the Florida Keys. No pretense here, just easygoing people with a passion for life and living it to the fullest with their friends.

The Half Shell has been in business on the Historic Key West waterfront since the early 70s and naturally became a favorite of captains and locals due to its central location and being surrounded by the Key West commercial fishing fleet. The same holds true today, as well as being a favorite dining destination for tourists and locals alike.

As you head toward the Half Shell Raw Bar, you can see the seafood being unloaded from the day's catch into the Half Shell Fish Market. They own their own seafood market, which supplies all of their needs plus their sister restaurants, therefore ensuring the freshest and finest quality products are always available. In fact, it is the only restaurant in town that owns its seafood market.

Walk into the bar, and you'll see the extensive draft beer taps, a large sailfish sculpture, and license plates from all over the world covering the walls. The well-worn barstools provide an inviting place to sit and chill with your favorite beverage as you recount the day's events with friends and plan new adventures. The Half Shell is a mecca beckoning to those looking to experience the cool and easygoing Caribbean lifestyle just like Chesney sings about in his songs.

The Half Shell Raw Bar is the original Key West fish house and offers such mouthwatering delights as broiled garlic oysters, fish and chips, steamed middleneck clams, chilled Key West peel-and-eat shrimp, and one of its specialties: authentic conch ceviche. Just imagine dining on the freshest seafood around while looking out over emerald-green waters and the golden Key West sunset.

Why not enjoy one of their signature drinks as the sun goes down? Try the Bayou Bloody Mary made with a jalapeno-infused vodka, homemade Bloody Mary mix, and old bay seasoning on the rim, served with a celery stalk and a peel-and-eat shrimp. The Oyster Shooter contains a shucked oyster, jalapeno-infused vodka, horseradish and cocktail sauce all in a souvenir shot glass. Looking for something more exotic? Then try the Voodoo Juice, a special blend of four flavored rums with a tropical fruit juice blend. Who knows...you might even strike up a conversation with one of Key West's leading charter captains and book yourself a fishing trip for the next day. Many of the local fishermen frequent the bar at Happy Hour, which is daily from 4:30 pm till 6:30 pm and features two-for-one specials.

If you're looking for a true Key West original and not the same old cookie-cutter establishment, amble on over to the Half Shell Raw Bar. They have all the ingredients for a special Old Key West experience...the only thing missing is you.

THE HALF SHELL RAW BAR ON THE KEY WEST WATERFRONT.
SUPPLIED BY HALF SHELL RAW BAR

6

MARGARITAVILLE

500 Duval Street
(305) 292-1435
Open daily 11:00 am – 12:00 am
www.margaritavillekeywest.com

Margaritaville is a place where it's always summer, the beer is ice-cold, and you can drop in any time of the year and enjoy a laid-back afternoon at the "beach." Grab a cheeseburger off the grill with fries and try a margarita from their signature blenders. Margaritaville's menu runs the gamut from appetizers, soups and salads, sandwiches, entrees, and, of course, a variety of cheeseburgers. Dive into their drink menu, which includes more than 10 varieties of margaritas, shooters, boat drinks, a multitude of beers including Land Shark, and a full wine list. The drink list draws inspiration from some of Jimmy Buffett's songs including names such as the Last Mango in Paris Margarita, Coastal Confession Boat Drink, and Back to the Island Sangria.

In business in Key West since 1985, the Margaritaville Store first opened at 4 Lands End Village and offered the T-shirts, beads, and trinkets that Buffett fans came in search of. When the store first opened, there was no restaurant or bar, and if you've ever listened to Jimmy Buffett, you know that he is famous for a couple of songs that refer to food and drink, namely cheeseburgers and margaritas.

Realizing that these integral appetites were going unsatisfied and also that they were quickly outgrowing their building, the Margaritaville Store moved to its present site at 500 Duval Street in the former SH Kress building where it was joined by the Margaritaville Cafe.

At the December 1987 opening of the Margaritaville Cafe on Duval Street, Jimmy Buffett quipped, "When I started out playing bars in this town, all I wanted was enough money to buy a boat I could sail away on if success faded. The other alternative was to buy my own bar so I could hire myself and just keep singing. Welcome to Margaritaville!" And as they say, the rest is history. Key West is the site of the first successful Margaritaville, and my, how the empire has grown since its humble beginnings as a T-shirt shop. The Margaritaville label now graces hotels, resorts and casinos, as well as restaurants across the country and the Caribbean.

Contrary to popular belief, Jimmy Buffett still goes down to the Keys every once in a while. Most recently, he was in town for the Key West Literary Seminar in January 2014. He also recorded his latest album, *Songs from St. Somewhere*, at his recording studio in Key West, and whose location I am sworn to keep secret.

You may or may not run into Jimmy on your visit to Key West, but you will definitely find a good time at Margaritaville.

ERNEST HEMINGWAY AND JOSIE "SLOPPY JOE" RUSSELL TOAST A SUCCESSFUL FISHING TRIP.
PUBLIC DOMAIN

SLOPPY JOE'S

201 Duval Street
(305) 294-5717
Monday thru Saturday 9:00 am – 4:00 am
Sunday 12:00 pm – 4:00 am
www.sloppyjoes.com

Located at the corner of Duval and Greene Streets since 1937, Sloppy Joe's has been at the top of the list in Key West bar lore. The official opening of Sloppy Joe's came with the repeal of prohibition on December 5, 1933, a short distance down Greene Street, which paved the way for Joe "Josie" Russell to open his first legitimate bar under the name of the Blind Pig.

Previously, Russell had been one of a group of Key West entrepreneurs who operated illegal speakeasies. A short time later, the bar changed names and became the Silver Slipper with the addition of a dance floor. It was with the third and final name that the bar became Sloppy Joe's as we know it today. This name was chosen at the suggestion of a good friend and most favored patron, Ernest Hemingway. It was so named in honor of one of Ole Hem's favorite bars in Havana, Cuba, which was owned by Jose Garcia. Hemingway was a good friend and fishing buddy of Josie Russell and a daily customer of the bar. Every afternoon after he had spent his morning writing, he would walk down to Sloppy Joe's, that is if he wasn't out on another offshore fishing adventure with the proprietor.

Originally located a short walk down Greene Street, it moved from its location due to the exorbitant rent increase of one dollar per week. Legend has it that the bar never really closed. Around midnight, the bar patrons simply picked up their drinks and all of the furniture in the bar and moved down to 201 Duval Street where service resumed without interruption.

Today, Sloppy Joe's is a legendary destination that everyone seeks out upon arriving in Key West. The good times start when the doors swing open at 9:00 am daily and noon on Sundays. Serving a diverse menu of Caribbean-American, it also includes bar favorites such as burgers, sandwiches, and salads. Be sure to wash down your delicious meals with one of SJ's generous signature drinks such as the Sloppy Rita, Frozen Bacardi Light Rum Runner, Sloppy Mojito, or Papa Dobles (Papa's favorite!).

Ever the Key West destination, its ceiling fans still spin just as in Hemingway's day. Speaking of Hemingway Days, there is a festival every July in Key West centered around Ernest Hemingway and his birthday on July 21. The renowned Hemingway Days Festival features exciting events such as an internationally recognized short story competition, storytelling contest, and Marlin Fishing Tournament. Sloppy Joe's plays a major part during the festival by sponsoring the Hemingway Look-Alike Contest. In fact, the Hemingway Days Festival was spawned at Sloppy Joe's in 1981.

Year round, you'll find musical entertainment on stage starting at noon and running into the evening. Stop by Joe's Tap Room if sports is your thing and watch NFL or College Football games on NFL Sunday Ticket and ESPN Game Plan. Also, watch games on NBA League Pass, ESPN Full Court, NHL Center Ice, and MLB Extra Innings. Whether you arrive by car, plane or ship, get down to Sloppy Joe's and make a great start to your trip.

SLOPPY JOES AT THE CORNER OF DUVAL AND GREENE STREETS SINCE 1937 AND STILL
GOING STRONG! SUPPLIED BY SLOPPY JOES'S

THE LATE, GREAT PATRIARCH OF CAPTAIN TONY'S, CAPTAIN TONY TARRACINO.
PHOTO CREDIT: ROB O'NEAL

CAPTAIN TONY'S SALOON

428 Greene Street
(305) 294-1838
Open daily 10:00 am – 2:00 am
www.capttonyssaloon.com

Housed in a building dating back to 1851, this bar has a history almost as colorful as its namesake, Captain Tony Tarracino. This site has served as an ice house in the days before electricity came to the Keys and also as the city morgue. Home to Key West's "Hanging Tree," it was the site of over 15 deaths including mostly pirates and one woman. This woman came to be known as the infamous "lady in blue" and it is said that her spirit still haunts Captain Tony's to this day.

In the 1890s, it housed a telegraph station where the news of the battleship Maine explosion in Cuba was received. Later, in the early 1900s, it served as a cigar factory, and during prohibition it was a speakeasy called the Blind Pig, which served up gambling, women, and bootleg rum called Hoover Gold.

Most notably, this is the original site of Sloppy Joe's, which is famous for being Ernest Hemingway's favorite daily watering hole in Key West. Opened by Joe "Josie" Russell in 1933 after the end of prohibition, it served as a spot for rest, storytelling, and occasional drama on the local Key West stage. It was only after a dispute over a rent increase of one dollar per week and a clause in the lease stating that all fixtures must stay if he ended the lease, that he decided to move the bar in the middle of the night, customers and fixtures included, to its present day location at the corner of Duval and Greene Streets. An interesting side note is that Hemingway insisted on claiming the bar's urinal in the move and relocated it to his home at 907 Whitehead Street, where it can still be seen today and is used as a watering trough for his beloved six-toed cats.

In 1958, the bar was purchased by Tony Tarrancino, a New Jersey transplant who had originally come to Key West for his "health." The story is told that Tony had been very successful with the horses out at the Garden State Race Track. He and his brothers figured out that they could get the results of the races with their dad's new TV before the bookies could, and they were winning a bundle. When the mob got wind of this, they took Tony on a little "one-way ride" to the landfill and left him for dead after a good beating. When Tony woke up the next day, he figured it would be better for his longevity if he left town. He headed south and came all the way down to Key West where he started a new life.

Captain Tony worked as a shrimper, charter boat captain, and even mayor of Key West but is known far and wide for his Saloon at 428 Greene Street. Captain Tony passed away in 2008, but his spirit lives on. His bar has changed little and still has ladies' bras on its ceiling. Business cards fill the posts around the bar and every barstool is painted with the name of a famous person who not only sat on it but also was a regular at the bar. There's live entertainment every afternoon and a live band every night and always a great crowd of locals and tourists alike.

Captain Tony's has become an institution in Key West and a must-visit destination on your itinerary. Come by and have one of their signature drinks and spend the afternoon. You'll be glad you did.

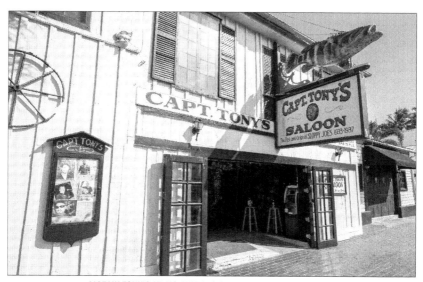

CAPTAIN TONY'S AT 428 GREENE STREET, JUST OFF DUVAL STREET.
PHOTO CREDIT: FOTOLUMINATE

THE SCHOONER WHARF BAR

202 William Street
(305) 292-3302
Open daily 7:00 am – 4:00 am
www.schoonerwharf.com

Often referred to as "a last little piece of Old Key West," and voted the Best Locals Bar six years in a row, you can't go wrong when you choose the Schooner Wharf. According to the bar's website, it was originally located on the Schooner Diamante and its top shelf liquor was kept in the top drawer of the file cabinet behind the bar. The Schooner has since been relocated and expanded on shore into a neighboring building and a second-story deck which overlooks the historic Key West waterfront and its yachts and sailboats.

A favorite of the Beach Boys, Al Jardine, it was also the choice watering hole of treasure salvor Mel Fisher, a legend in his own right. The Schooner's rustic charm and locals flavor appealed to this local hero who sought out and found the treasure of the *Atocha*—full of gems, coins, and precious metals—in the waters off the Florida Keys. Charles Kuralt, the late CBS journalist, when referring to the Schooner stated, "this must be the center of the universe."

With its waterfront location and nautical motif, you'll enjoy some of the freshest seafood around. Fresh stone crab claws, peel-and-eat shrimp, fresh-shucked oysters, and, of course, conch chowder and fritters, are among the local seafood delicacies on the menu in the galley. For the land lovers of your crew, you'll find a bountiful assortment of appetizers, burgers, chicken, soups, and salads.

The Schooner Wharf offers three different happy hours throughout the day: from 8:00 am till noon, 5:00 to 7:00 pm and 2:00 to 4:00 am. Check out their extensive frozen and tropical drink menu, as well as a bountiful bevy of beers: www.schoonerwharf.com/pdf/drink-menu-2012.pdf.

The Schooner Wharf is an active part of the community and sponsors over 30 events throughout the year such as the Lighted

Boat Parade in December, the Minimal Regatta over the Memorial Day weekend, Wrecker's Cup Race Series, Barbecue Cook-off, Chili Cook-off, and one of the Keys favorite local events, the Battle of the Bars. Entertainment abounds and is sure to keep you captivated into the evening.

Frank Everhart is the in-house magician and has been wowing patrons for the past 16 years with his up-close magic and sleight of hand. He performs 5 days a week so be sure to come any evening Wednesday thru Sunday with magic commencing at 9:00 pm. If it's music that gets you started, you'll find a variety of melodic entertainment starting every day at noon and running late into the night. Be sure to check the website, www.schoonerwharf.com/entertainment.htm, for the latest schedule of entertainers coming to the Schooner Wharf stage.

THE SCHOONER WHARF BAR ON THE KEY WEST WATERFRONT.
PHOTO CREDIT: MARK LEE

HOG'S BREATH SALOON

400 Front Street
(305) 296-4222
Open daily 10:00 am – 2:00 am
www.hogsbreath.com/keywest

The world-famous Hog's Breath Saloon has been serving its thirsty patrons for more than 25 years in the heart of Key West and a stone's throw to the waterfront and Mallory Square. Don't let its biker bar atmosphere scare you as all are welcome at the Hog.

Not to drop names, but recently, in March 2013, Kenny Chesney chose to kick off his latest US tour here at the Hog's Breath. He held an impromptu concert billed at Kegs in the Keys and played for a crowd of about five thousand, who were shoulder to shoulder on the patio, bar, and spilling into the street as he wowed the crowd in one of his favorite locations to be, Key West.

Originally started in 1976 by Jerry Dorminy in Ft. Walton Beach, FL as somewhere to hang out with his friends after a hard day of sailing and fishing, he branched out in 1988 and thus was born the Hog's Breath in Key West. He was looking for somewhere known for its watersports and fishing like Fort Walton, and Key West was the perfect fit. It has great fishing and diving, and the nightlife has an energy all of its own. Since its inception, the Hog's Breath has been popular with the locals and the place where tourists go to try and fit in and taste a little bit of the local flavor.

It offers a full menu of favorites including appetizers such as Buffalo Hogs Wings, Bahamian Conch Chowder, and Seafood Sampler. Its entrees are crowd-pleasing favorites such as a full range of sandwiches and dinner portions of mahi-mahi, shrimp, or crab. Don't forget the Raw Bar where you'll find oysters by the dozen, shrimp, and stone crab (when in season). Also, try one of their signature drinks such as the Hog Snort, the Hogarita, or Havana Hog Punch. Prices are reasonable and portions are generous. Come as you are and blend in with the locals at the Hog's Breath.

THE GREEN PARROT

601 Whitehead Street
(305) 294-6133
Open daily 10:00 am – 4:00 am
Happy Hour daily 4:00 pm – 7:00 pm
www.greenparrot.com

Green Parrot, the name conjures up images in your mind of something colorful, tropical, and certainly out of the ordinary. It usually inhabits exotic tropical islands loaded with beautiful wildlife and is often surrounded by emerald-green waters. Sounds like you could also be describing the Green Parrot Bar located just off the main drag at the corner of Southard and Whitehead Streets in Key West.

The Green Parrot has been referred to by *Playboy* magazine as "the definitive Key West saloon" and was named in their top twenty bars of America. It has also garnered a certificate of excellence from the respected Trip Advisor website. With a timeless atmosphere and an open air feel, it may seem that very little has changed since the building was occupied by its first resident.

Originally constructed in 1890, the building served as the grocery store of local merchant Antonio Sanchez, as well as the boyhood home of renowned folk artist Mario Sanchez, Antonio's grandson. The transition to saloon occurred in the 1940s when the Brown Derby opened to serve the thirsty navy submarine crews who were stationed in Key West. Sailors who were stationed here and returned in later years have remarked that they can barely find the former navy base but felt right at home once they got back to the "old Brown Derby."

The Navy left in the early seventies and so did the name, with the venerable saloon returning as the Green Parrot. Key West was quickly becoming a mecca for artists, bikers, free spirits, and otherwise nonconformists. The Parrot became a place where old sailors and old hippies were welcome and could be found side by side at the bar.

Music has always figured prominently in the appeal of the Green Parrot. Starting in the days of Antonio Sanchez, local Latin musicians would have informal jam sessions, called *descargasin,* in the back room of his grocery store. Today, the Green Parrot offers some of the hottest performers around and has been recognized by Zagat Survey as the number one music venue in South Florida. Any given weekend, you can find a nationally recognized touring band performing on the stage, and during the week, the jukebox cranks out the tunes as you enjoy a game of darts, pool or pinball, and some complimentary popcorn.

If you've worked up a thirst, try one of their signature drinks, the Green Parrot Root Beer Barrel, made with Root Beer Schnapps and beer. The Green Parrot is known for its great drinks and ice-cold beer and you never know whom you might meet sitting on the barstool next to you. For a unique experience and a chance to rub elbows with tourists and locals alike, come on over and have a drink at the Green Parrot tonight.

YOU'LL FIND THE GREEN PARROT, JUST 1 BLOCK OVER FROM DUVAL.
PHOTO CREDIT: MARK LEE

THE PORCH

429 Caroline Street
(305) 517-6358
Open daily 11:00 am – 4:00 am
www.theporchkw.com

The Porch is truly a hidden gem of Key West, found just outside the fray of Duval at 429 Caroline Street. Opened in July 2010 by well-known Key West author, Chris Shultz, and Keith St. Peter, it is housed in the historic Porter Mansion. This Victorian structure is so named for Dr. Joseph Porter, its former owner and resident, who is said to have been born and died in the same upstairs room. As the story goes, Dr. Porter, the first native-born Key West physician was also the state of Florida's first medical officer. One of the most common diseases of his time was malaria and when his patients died, he would often put dimes on their eyes. His ghost still reportedly inhabits the Porch today and is said to throw glasses about the room and leave dimes on the bar upon occasion. Originally constructed in 1838, the Porter Mansion has been on the US National Register of Historic Places since 1973.

The Porch is a mecca for the craft beer aficionado and offers over 18 drafts and 50-plus bottles of the finest beers from US and international sources. The draft beer list is refreshed on a regular basis to offer the beer lover a chance to savor new experiences and keep up with the latest brews. They also have an extensive wine list with 12 wines by the glass and a well-appointed selection of over 70 bottles to drink or carry home for later. Of course, their friendly and knowledgeable staff is always there to steer you in the right direction. Noted to be a locals kind of place and very popular with the off-duty bartenders of the island, you'll always have plenty of advice as to the best and latest beers to try. If you feel like taking a walk outside, it's okay to grab a chair and enjoy your brew or fruit of the vine al fresco on the large and inviting wraparound porch.

I will only quote a few of the reviews found on the Facebook site of the Porch lest I cause a stampede of bar goers and totally screw up the ambiance and casual appeal of this place. Past patrons have said, "great vibes, good people and best of all good beer," and "perfect spot to get away from the madness," and my personal favorite, "delicious beer will magically appear." The Porch has been featured in the *New York Times, Southern Living,* and *Gun and Garden.* With reviews like that, why are you still reading? I'm on my way now to the Porch!

HOUSED IN THE HISTORIC PORTER MANSION, THE PORCH HAS THE BEST CRAFT BEER SELECTION IN TOWN.
PHOTO CREDIT: MARK LEE

THE CHART ROOM

1 Duval Street
(305) 296-4600
Open daily 4:30 pm – 2:00 am
Happy Hour 4:30 pm – 6:00 pm
www.pierhouse.com/Dining/chart_room.asp

On its website, the Pier House Resort refers to the Chart Room as "a weird little bar trapped inside a luxury resort." It has been said by many that the Chart Room is such an integral and beloved part of Key West that the Pier House has literally developed around it.

Since 1968, with a quirky character all of its own, the Chart Room Bar has stood the test of time at Key West's waterfront. Once the regular watering hole of literary luminaries such as Tennessee Williams, Truman Capote, and Hunter S. Thompson, it holds a special place in the hearts of locals and guests of the Pier House Resort. Local legend has it that Jimmy Buffett crafted his laid-back tropical style of music by playing for drinks in the Chart Room in his early Key West days. He polished his style while singing for treasure divers, beach goers, politicians, and friends. In fact, both Jimmy Buffett and Bob Marley played their first gigs here.

Carol Shaugnessy of the Florida Keys News Bureau interviewed Chris Robinson, former Chart Room bartender, and this was his take on Key West and the role that the Chart Room played. "Politicos ran the government largely from the Chart Room Bar, pot smugglers were admired as romantic outlaws, and local treasure hunters drank rum with Pulitzer-winning escapees from the literary mainstream." Long since retired from his bartending days and sharing adventures with the likes of Jimmy Buffett and Hunter Thompson, Robinson now spends his days on the local waters working as a fishing guide on his own boat.

Key West has changed a lot since its renegade days of the 70s and you probably would have better luck finding the local politicians at City Hall. However, the Chart Room still holds court on the waterfront for tourists and locals alike. It's open daily from 4:30 pm till 2:00 am with Happy Hour from 4:30 pm till 6:00 pm. Come by, grab a barstool, and have a drink, and enjoy its free popcorn, peanuts and hot dogs. Just don't ask for one of those blender drinks with the cute little umbrellas. They don't have a blender or umbrellas...just cool drinks, great company, and a good time.

RUMORED TO BE KENNY CHESNEY'S YACHT, THIS GREY BEAUTY WAS CRUISING JUST OFF MALLORY SQUARE.
PHOTO CREDIT: MARK LEE

HOG FISH BAR AND GRILL

6810 Front Street Stock Island, FL 33040
(305) 293-4041
Monday thru Saturday 11:00 am – 11:00 pm
Sunday 8:00 am – 11:00 pm
www.hogfishbar.com

Take a short little drive, just off Key West over Cow Channel Bridge, down Front Street, past a row of rusty old trailers and you'll stumble upon a part of the Keys that time has forgotten. Here in Safe Harbor Marina, you'll find the Hog Fish Bar and Grill, where locals bring their out-of-town friends to show them what Key West used to be like before development came.

Situated on the waterfront next to the marina that is rumored to have served as the headquarters for the Bay of Pigs Invasion of Cuba in the 1960s, the Hogfish serves fresh local seafood and strong drinks. The establishment takes its name from the delicious but often hard to come by fish of the same moniker. The motto around Key West on hogfish—a flaky, delicate, white-fleshed fish—is, "we have it when we have it." It's native to these waters, but it's hard to come by—not only does it have to be speared by a diver, but it's also seasonal.

If you like seafood, you'll find no fresher. Dine on peel-and-eat shrimp and drink ice-cold beer as you watch the shrimp boats pull back into the marina, freshly loaded with the catch of the day. Sitting at your waterfront table or tiki-style booth, you'll have the perfect perch to witness all the comings and goings along the waterfront and the perfect vantage point to welcome the evening's arrival as the sun moves slowly out of view.

The Hogfish Bar and Grill has been featured on the *Today* show with Matt Laurer and Al Roker. It was also on a segment of Adam Richman's *Man vs. Food*. A favorite of the locals for its Old Key West appeal, it has attracted such notables as Jimmy Buffett, Paula Dean, and Vanilla Ice. Do yourself a favor and drive on over to the Hog Fish Bar and Grill. You'll find easy to follow directions on their website.

23

THE BULL AND WHISTLE BAR

224 Duval Street
(305) 296-4565
Monday thru Saturday 10:00 am – 4:00 am
Sunday 12:00 pm – 4:00 am
www.bullkeywest.com

The Bull is the oldest open-air bar in Old Town Key West and can be found at the corner of Duval and Caroline Streets. It harkens back to Key West's rough seafaring days and a good time can always be found here. Sit and while away the day as you sip on one of your favorite beverages and people-watch as the folks stroll by just outside your window. Enjoy the hand-painted murals that can be found on the walls surrounding you, rich with a pictorial of Key West's golden days and historical residents.

If you're looking to kick things up a notch, then walk a few steps up to the Whistle Bar, which is found on the second story just above the Bull. The Whistle offers some of the same fare as the Bull, only with a better view. Take a bird's eye perspective of Old Key West as you peer over the railing of its second-story balcony. Feel free to pull up a barstool or stand at its wrought iron railing and spend a relaxing afternoon or evening sipping on your favorite drink.

Finally, if you're feeling adventurous or have worked up enough courage, you may want to wander up to the third and final floor of the Bull and Whistle, which is known as the Garden of Eden. And yes, it is just what you may be thinking, this is the only Key West's clothing-optional roof-garden bar where clothing is not required and cameras are not welcome. Called "the best-kept secret in Key West" by *Rolling Stone* magazine, the Garden of Eden offers live bands, body painting, drink specials, and one of the best views in town. Get there and stay until dusk and participate in their signature event, the Naked Sunset.

You'll be sure to have an unforgettable day whether you visit one or all of their bars so come by today and let one of their friendly bartenders serve you and enjoy your stay.

THE MULTI TIERED BULL AND WHISTLE IS ACTUALLY THREE BARS UNDER ONE ROOF.
PHOTO CREDIT: MARK LEE

THE SMOKIN TUNA IS IN THE HEART OF OLD TOWN KEY WEST ON CHARLES STREET.
PHOTO CREDIT: MARK LEE

THE SMOKING TUNA SALOON

4 Charles Street
(305) 517-6350
Bar open daily 10:00 am – 2:00 am
Raw Bar and Restaurant 11:00 am – 10:00 pm
www.smokingtunasaloon.com

The Smoking Tuna Saloon is new to the island and is known for its great live music and raw bar. Located just off Duval on Charles Street, you can enjoy some of the best bands around in a relaxed atmosphere. Half of the bar is covered and the remainder is located outside in a tree-covered tropical patio.

The Smoking Tuna is a sponsor of the Key West Songwriters Festival, which is held in May and features over a hundred of the top songwriters in the country. Musicians and songwriters from all over the United States converge on the island of Key West for a week of great music and entertainment. This unique event gives the audience a chance to put a face to the music, so to speak, and further immerse themselves in the music they might otherwise never hear. It also gives the songwriter a chance to tell his story as it may never otherwise be heard as, more often than not, their creations are turned into hits by more famous musical entertainers.

The Smoking Tuna is, of course, famous for what else...its tuna. For starters, why not try some of their signature Smoking Tuna Dip served with tortilla chips, and I hear the Conch Fritters are great also. They offer a tasty mahi-mahi sandwich, which can be had blackened or jerked. The Smoking Tuna also offers a full half-pound hamburger for those with a big appetite, grilled to order and served with fries. Of course, they offer a full list of drinks sure to quench your thirst. Just head down Duval and veer onto Charles, and you'll find the Smoking Tuna, and a smoking good time.

THE RUM BARREL

528 Front Street
(305) 292-7862
Open daily 11:00 am until close
www.rumbarrel.com

Step into the Rum Barrel, and you'll find yourself in a pirate's paradise in the heart of Old Key West. Launched in 2006 by the highly successful entrepreneur Pat Croce, the nautical themed Rum Barrel exudes that seafaring atmosphere that is engrained in Old Key West and features over 150 of the world's finest rums as well as a vast array of specialty and craft choices.

Executive chef and director of operations, Michael Shultz, brings his own flair to the restaurant and draws upon his diverse blend of experience in the culinary field. Starting at the age of 14 at the Lobster House in Cape May, New Jersey, he has also worked as a chef for the Hollywood producer/director, M. Night Shyamalan as well as some of the eastern seaboard's finest restaurants. It was after a vacation in Key West that he made his decision to make it his home.

With Pat Croce being the former president of the Philadelphia 76ers, the Rum Barrel is rich with the Philly influence. In fact, it is the southernmost Philly sports bar and is renowned for its legendary tailgates, fervent fans, and the go-to place for all things Philly, including its famous cheese steaks. The Rum Barrel uses the recipe from Geno's Steaks, a South Philly tradition, which has been featured on the *Food Network* and many other media outlets.

Located just a block from the waterfront, the Rum Barrel's upper deck provides an impressive panoramic view of Old Key West and in the distance, the emerald waters of the Gulf of Mexico. With nightly entertainment and daily specials, its outdoor stage has even seen a performance by the dynamic *American Idol* performer, Bo Bice.

Happy hour starts at 4:00 pm and runs till 7:00 pm daily except for football season, when it is Monday thru Friday. The Barrel offers two-for-one domestic drafts and bottles, and premium well drinks with a full five-dollar Key West Happy Hour menu. They also have a full menu, which offers a bounty of appetizers and full meals ranging from seafood to steaks. Plan on sailing down to the Rum Barrel today and have your own swashbuckling pirate experience.

LOUIE'S BACKYARD

700 Waddell Avenue
(305) 294-1061
www.louiesbackyard.com

The first thing that I learned in real estate was location, location, location, and that is but one of the many attributes that draws you to Louie's Backyard. This little piece of paradise is situated on a waterfront lot overlooking the azure green waters of the Atlantic Ocean where Waddell Avenue meets the south shore of Key West. Its Afterdeck Bar is an open-air platform, which not only features one of the best sunset views in town but in the evening transforms into a romantic rendezvous, resplendent with the lights of Key West dancing on the shimmering water. However, if its beauty and location draws you there, its fabulous food, wine, and service keep you coming back for more, time after time.

In 1971, this picturesque Victorian-styled oceanfront home belonging to Louie Signorelli was transformed into Louie's Backyard. It was an intimate establishment that seated only 12 patrons and was serviced by one waiter. Its daily receipts were kept in a cigar box. In its early days, one could easily bump into one of the locals such as Jimmy Buffett, Thomas McGuane, or even Hunter S. Thompson, on any given day. Jimmy lived just over the fence in one of the upstairs neighboring apartments. In 1983, the property changed hands and was carefully renovated by the new owners who took great care to observe the historical integrity of the structure during the process. Due to their diligence and attention to detail, Louie's Backyard is now on the National Register of Historical Places.

Chef Doug Shook has been working his magic in the kitchen of Louie's for over 26 years and uses a blend of fresh local seafood, fruits and vegetables. The vegetables are grown by Island Farms especially for Louie's and the fruits come freshly picked from Mr. Wong. The lobster and Key West pink shrimp are so fresh that they were probably swimming in the local waters just yesterday. If you

29

fancy something besides seafood, Louie's has plenty of other choices such as choice steak, heirloom pork, lamb, and free-range chicken.

If you don't have a reservation, no worries, go to the Upper Deck, Louie's Wine Bar. It has a magnificent wine list that can be enjoyed by the glass and provides what some consider the best panoramic view of the ocean on Key West. They also serve a variety of foods to complement your wine choice, as well as an assortment of cheeses. They are open evenings from 5:00 to 10:00 pm, Tuesday thru Saturday.

For an unforgettable feast for the eyes and stomach, plan an evening at Louie's Backyard.

LOUIE'S BACKYARD IS LOCATED IN A BEAUTIFULLY RESTORED WATERFRONT HOUSE ON WADDELL AVENUE.
PHOTO CREDIT: MARK LEE

FAT TUESDAY

305 Duval Street
(305) 296-9373
Open daily 10:00 am until close
Happy Hour Monday thru Friday 4:00 pm –7:00 pm
www.fattuesdaykeywest.com

Mardi Gras has been running year round since 1990 at Fat Tuesday in Key West. Located at 305 Duval Street, Fat Tuesday is an open-air bar, which is famous for its potent frozen daiquiris with colorful names such as the 190 Octane, Cat 5 Hurricane, and Violet Behavior. It also offers a full-service bar with mixed drinks, beer, jello shots, and, of course, Key West Margaritas.

In addition to the eight large flat-screen TVs found throughout, you'll also find a DJ spinning the hottest music over a pumping sound system to fuel your party from 9:00 pm to close every day. Fat Tuesday also hosts parties coinciding with special events happening in Key West throughout the year such as Spring Break, Lobsterfest, Hemingway Days, Parrot Heads, Bike Week, Powerboat Races, and Fantasy Fest.

If you've ever considered renting a bar for an event, you have the flexibility of either holding a private party on the back deck or renting out the entire facility for your special event. Fat Tuesday offers a delicious menu of appetizers to serve at your function and help make it a success.

Stop by today and beat the heat with one of their signature frozen drinks but be careful of brain freeze. Their bartenders can give you several tips on how to avoid it and have a great time.

IRISH KEVIN'S BAR

211 Duval Street
(305) 292-1262
Monday thru Sunday 10:00 am –2:30 am
www.irishkevins.com

Irish Kevin's Bar opened in 1998 by, strangely enough, three guys named Kevin. It was the musician in the bunch whose first name was borrowed and also given a nod to his Irish heritage. The Kevins were pioneers in the late nineties when they opened their bar in Key West that featured live music and entertainers from open to close. Irish Kevin's chose a building that seems a natural for its purpose. It was once a Budweiser warehouse and later turned into the former location of a brewpub. When the Kevins took over, they held on to the brew tanks for a while before moving them out in favor of the gift shop and a private balcony.

Irish Kevin's is known by the trademarked slogan: "I came, I drank, I don't remember," so how could you go wrong. It is famous for its friendly party atmosphere where the performers joke and cajole the crowd and fully encourage interaction and sing-alongs. The musicians usually perform five days a week with the performer changing every four hours, so if you don't like what you hear now, stick around and it's sure to change sooner or later. A wide variety of music can be heard from their stage including modern, 50s, country and, of course, Irish tunes. I've heard that a few famous faces have graced Irish Kevin's and possibly sung a tune or two including

32

Toby Keith, Rhett Akins, Lee Brice, and Jamie Johnson.

Irish Kevin's not only serves great drinks including Guinness and Irish whiskeys but also offers a full menu of super bar food. The Gunny is said to be one of the favorites and is a sandwich comprised of smoked gouda cheese combined with smoked turkey and topped with their signature spicy mangrove mustard, mayo, lettuce, and tomato on sweet Hawaiian bread. You may want to try one of their tasty appetizers with it such as the tater tot nachos. These nachos are made of tater tots topped with melted cheese, bacon, and jalapenos, wow!

Irish Kevin's celebrates St. Patrick's in a big way. The weekend before St. Patrick's is a full-blown celebration that leads up to the biggest Irish holiday of the year. On Saturday, Irish Kevin's opens at 7:00 am to allow its patrons to warm up for the IK5K. The IK5K includes a costume contest, free drinks, breakfast, and a T-shirt for all participants. On St. Patrick's eve there is a countdown to midnight that includes a balloon drop as twelve strikes, and then on St. Patrick's Day, the bar opens again at 7:00 am for a free breakfast and all those eager beavers who want to get a jump on the day's festivities.

You don't have to wait until St. Patty's Day to have a good time at Irish Kevin's. They're open every day from 10:00 am till 2:30 am, serving up fun, food, and drink. Come on over today.

ST. PATRICK'S IS IRISH KEVIN'S BIGGEST EVENT OF THE YEAR BUT A GREAT DESTINATION YEAR ROUND.
PHOTO CREDIT: MARK LEE

JACK FLATS

509.5 Duval Street
(305) 294-7955
Open daily 11:00 am till late
www.jackflatskw.com

On a recent Saturday afternoon in November, my wife and I had just finished a successful trip to Margaritaville and were looking for someplace to watch the UGA Bulldog college football game. As I was walking down the sidewalk on Duval across from Parrothead Central, I looked into Jack Flats and saw nothing but screen after screen of college football games, all on flat screen TVs as far as the eye could see. Little did I know that I had just stumbled upon the next bar that would make it into the *Ultimate Key West Bar Guide*. We spent several hours cheering our favorite team and enjoyed some of the best hot wings and sandwiches in Key West. Jack Flats is located in the heart of Duval Street in Old Town Key West at 509½ Duval Street, almost directly across from Margaritaville.

For the sports enthusiast, I can think of no better place to be. Jack Flats has 19 big-screen TVs on which to enjoy watching your favorite game, coupled with a delicious menu. To say that their portions are generous would be an understatement. My plate was piled high with a mound of tots the height of Everest, and the sandwiches are large enough to share or satisfy the hardiest appetite. They have an extensive appetizer menu with crowd-pleasing favorites such as

Buffalo Wings, Jack's Nachos, and US 1 Sliders. The local seafood supply lends itself to such selections as Buffalo or Coconut Shrimp, Jack's Fish Bites, and Blackened Mahi Sliders. Jack's has six different salads to choose from, and you can choose from a variety of sandwiches. They have great burgers, and seafood sandwiches made with dolphin, shrimp, or grouper. Each sandwich comes with either French fries or sweet potato fries or you can have a mound of tater tots for just an extra dollar. Try one of their eight Blue Plate specials, ranging from Jack's Meatloaf to Jack's Sirloin steak, grilled to order with mash potatoes and broccoli. You'll also find more Blue Plate favorites such as Chicken Parm, Fish and Chips, Jack's Shepherd's Pie, and Margarita Chicken. Last, but certainly not least, make sure to save room for a piece of either their scrumptious Key Lime Pie or Chocolate Cake. If you are a sports enthusiast or just looking for some great food which is big on flavor and portion, you can't go wrong with Jack Flats.

Key West TOURS

KEY WEST GHOST HUNT

(305) 290-3451
Reservations taken daily from 10:00 am – 10:00 pm
Tours depart nightly rain or shine
www.keywestghosthunt.com

What do you get when you combine one of the most haunted cities in America with a one-of-a-kind, interactive paranormal experience? You get the Key West Ghost Hunt, the brainchild of noted author, entrepreneur, and Key West resident David L. Sloan.

Sloan started the original Key West ghost tours after relocating to the island in 1996. Before he came to town, ghost tours were pretty much unheard of in the United States, and after experiencing such a tour in Scotland, David knew that he wanted to start just such a tour.

David can actually trace his interests in ghosts and the supernatural back to his childhood in Philadelphia, where he would conduct his own ghost tours in several historic hotels that his grandfather managed. However, he credits his kindergarten teacher with really kindling the fires of his ghostly passion. He recounts that she would tell stories to the class about a Native American spirit that was haunting her house, and he knew he was really hooked the day she brought in a photograph of him for the class to see.

When he first moved to town, David was attempting to start his research on the ghosts of Key West but was meeting with little success until one fateful evening. He recalls that he was in his '84

39

Thunderbird when the ghost of a man in his mid-30s appeared in his car and encouraged him to "Go back to the library." He admits he was taken aback but did as the apparition bid and indeed returned to the library where he found that his luck was about to change. It was there where he met with a local historian, Tom Hambright, who directed him to an archive that was literally brimming with Key West's ghostly happenings. This research that Sloan did served as the beginnings of Key West's first ghost tour. He would later sell this successful tour business and embark on authoring a series of books about ghosts and help to establish tours in other cities. His tours and books have been featured on numerous cable channels including *The History Channel*, *Discovery Channel*, and *Travel Channel* in the US, and also international outlets such as the *BBC*.

In 2013, he started the venture that we know today as the Key West Ghost Hunt, and it is a product of the extensive research that has been done to this date. It continues to evolve as Sloan pursues his passion for research of the paranormal.

Always on the cutting edge of his field, Sloan has added the latest in ghost hunting technology to the tour. Each participant gets to experience and use items such as electromagnetic field detectors, divining rods, and laser thermometers. It is said that a ghostly presence can be felt by a sudden chill in the air, and temps in the 20s have been detected in balmy Key West as a ghost makes his presence known. When asked about a typical hunt, Sloan said that fascinating stories and dark history are guaranteed. It is also common to encounter the paranormal in the form of cold chills, people being poked and touched, ghostly sounds, and on rare occasions, an apparition. Key West is a hotbed of ghostly activity and is rife with stories of ghostly encounters around locations on the island such as the Ernest Hemingway Home, the Key West Lighthouse, and the Porter Mansion, which now houses a bar known as the Porch. Stories abound at the Porch that the ghost of Dr. Porter still visits to this day to toss wine glasses about and produces dimes from thin air.

Your ghostly adventure on the Key West Ghost Hunt starts every night of the week with a check-in at Kelly's Caribbean Bar, Grill, and

Brewery. From there, each person receives a piece of ghost detecting equipment, and the 90-minute walking tour of Key West's most haunted neighborhoods begins. The tour departs rain or shine, so call to make your reservations and be prepared to be entertained and amazed. Who knows, you might even have the fright of your life.

NOTED KEY WEST AUTHOR AND GHOST HUNTER DAVID SLOAN MESMERIZES GHOST TOUR PARTICIPANT.
PHOTO COURTESY OF KEY WEST GHOST HUNT.

TOOLS OF THE TRADE OF A GHOST HUNTER.
PHOTO COURTESY OF KEY WEST GHOST HUNT.

41

THE KEY WEST SCAVENGER HUNT

(305) 292-9994
www.keywesthunt.com

What do you get when you combine the fun of a bar crawl with the excitement of a scavenger hunt? That's what you find when you go on the Key West Scavenger Hunt. The classic scavenger hunt takes individual groups of visitors on a one-of-a-kind interactive tour of Old Key West. All are welcome to join in on this exciting adventure to compete against other teams or just play for points and great prizes.

Along the way, you'll gather interesting tidbits of trivia and history about Key West and visit some of its famous sites, landmarks, and hot spots. Each scavenger hunt lasts about three hours and culminates with the awards ceremony where the winners are announced and the prizes are bestowed.

The award-winning Southernmost Scavenger Hunt starts at the historic La Concha Crowne Plaza Hotel at 430 Duval Street. The La Concha is the perfect place to experience Duval Street and the best of Key West. As the tallest building on the island, the observation deck on the seventh floor allows you to enjoy a panoramic view of Key West. From the Atlantic to the Gulf of Mexico, this is one of the best spots to view the island that you will soon be exploring.

For more information, go the website or just call (305) 292-9994 to check on availability for this unbelievable quest.

CONCH TRAIN TOUR

303 Front Street
1-888-916-8687 (TOUR)
www.conchtourtrain.com

What began as a family business in the 1950s has grown into a Key West tradition and remains one of the most famous attractions in the state of Florida to this day. It's also one of the best ways to see the island and learn about its colorful history and characters. Their friendly and knowledgeable staff have delighted and entertained over 15 million visitors during its many years of operation.

Its world-famous black locomotives and yellow train cars can be seen crawling through Key West from 9:00 am to 4:30 pm daily with new tours departing every thirty minutes. These 90-minute tours are fun and educational, and you'll hear about some of Key West's famous former residents such as Ernest Hemingway, Mel Fisher, Jimmy Buffett, and even President Harry S. Truman. Of course, you'll also learn about Henry Flagler, the visionary who built the engineering masterpiece called the Overseas Railroad, which was the first completed in 1912 and connected the Florida mainland with the Keys before bridges were built for car travel to Key West.

The best way to catch the train is to head to the Front Street Station, purchase your ticket, and board the train, but you can also climb on at Flager Station or Truval Village if seats are available. It makes several stops along the way, which give the opportunity to get refreshments, go to the restroom, or do a little shopping. The tour encompasses many sites of interest such as the Hemingway Home and Museum, the Key West Lighthouse, Truman's Little White House, and the Southernmost Point. It's one of the best ways to see where things are in town and also find about our colorful past, so punch your ticket today and all aboard!

43

THE CONCH TRAIN IS FUN AND INFORMATIVE ROLLING HISTORY LESSON OF KEY WEST.
PHOTO COURTESY OF THE CONCH TRAIN TOUR.

GETTING THERE

I'm assuming you're sitting at home reading this and not in Key West because otherwise you would be out doing all the fun stuff, so let's talk about how to get there. There are many different ways to get to Key West. You can literally get there by land, air, or sea.

A road trip is always a good idea depending on how far you live from South Florida. If you're not from a subtropical area, the drive through the Keys will be a true experience as it's like a tour through an emerald paradise with a breathtaking vista around every corner. Just in case you fly or come by boat and miss this great experience, I'll give you a little glimpse of a drive through the Keys in a minute.

If you decide to fly, Key West has a great airport as does Marathon just up the road. You'll find a modern airport accessible either by connecting through Miami or in some cases, a direct flight.

If you have your own boat, it's a no-brainer, set sail for Key West. But if you don't have your own vessel, Key West is one of the most popular stops around on many of the cruise ship itineraries. If you're on the west coast of Florida, there is an express ferry from Fort Myers and Marco Island to Key West. Let's take a look at each of these choices so you can decide which fits you best!

RIDE FROM MIAMI TO KEY WEST

Just south of Miami, I-95 ends and becomes US 1, which runs all the way to Mile Marker Zero in Key West. As you motor southward, you see signs for attractions such as the Monkey Jungle and pass through towns with classy names like Princeton and Naranja. The farther you drive the urban landscape gradually gives way to the suburban until you finally feel as though you're leaving civilization behind at Florida City. Just before the left-hand turn to Card Sound

Road, you'll find the Last Chance Saloon, which welcomes according to its sign, "Friendly People Only!"

BE ON YOUR BEST BEHAVIOR IF YOU WANT TO BE SERVED HERE. THEY ONLY SERVE FRIENDLY PEOPLE AND THIS IS YOUR "LAST CHANCE." PHOTO CREDIT: MARK LEE

You leave behind the pine trees and occasional billboard and sail on through the scrubby, sandy flatland until shortly out the starboard window you see the flowing grassy plains of the Everglades National Park. The Everglades is the largest subtropical wilderness in the United States and is the natural habitat for rare and endangered species such as the manatee, American crocodile, and the Florida panther. It is at Manatee Creek where you leave the mainland and embark on your jaunt through the Keys. To your left, you see Pelican Cay Harbor just north of Key Largo. Key Largo is the largest and also the first Key that you encounter as you go down the Overseas Highway. The Overseas Highway was actually constructed over the roadbed of Henry Flagler's Overseas Railway, which was the southernmost line of his Florida East Coast Railway that linked mainland Florida with Key West in the early 1900s.

Key Largo is known as the "dive capital of the world," and provides numerous opportunities for scuba diving and snorkeling. Two of its main attractions are the John Pennekamp Coral Reef Park and the Key Largo National Marine Sanctuary. These protected waters provide a picturesque environment to enjoy the undersea beauty of

Florida's saltwater citizens. You can also see the *African Queen* in Key Largo, the boat that was featured in the Humphrey Bogart's movie from the 1950s of the same title.

Just a few miles down the road, you find Islamorada known as the Sports Fishing Capital of the world. If you need fishing tackle or just looking to take a break, check out the Worldwide Sportsman in Islamorada, one of my personal favorites places to go. Here you'll find one of the best outfitters in the Keys for saltwater tackle and accessories. Step inside the cavernous store, and you will also see what is known as the sister boat to Ernest Hemingway's *Pilar*, his beloved fishing yacht constructed by the Wheeler Shipyard in Brooklyn, New York, in the 1930s. Another one of my favorite things to do is celebrate the sunset at the Lorelei Restaurant and Cabana Bar on their beachfront seating area overlooking the Gulf of Mexico with my toes in the sand. You can't beat the views or the refreshments, and you will find the Lorelei around mile marker 82.

WORLDWIDE SPORTSMAN IS A GREAT OUTFITTER IN ISLAMORADA FOR SALT WATER FISHING GEAR.
COURTESY OF WORLDWIDE SPORTSMAN

THE SISTER BOAT TO ERNEST HEMINGWAY'S PILAR CAN BE SEEN INSIDE THE WORLDWIDE SPORTSMAN.
COURTESY OF WORLDWIDE SPORTSMAN

Resuming our journey to Key West, you pass through several more small keys until you reach the community of Marathon. Marathon is known as the family and boating destination of the Florida Keys and is one of its most marine-friendly cities with nearly 1,200 wet slips, 1,200 dry slips, and top-notch facilities to attract the transient cruiser. Another major attraction to Marathon is the Dolphin Research Center, a nonprofit organization dedicated to education, research, and caring for our marine animals and the environment. Now we're getting close as Key West is just a little more than 50 miles away. It is here at Marathon that we'll start across the Seven Mile Bridge—one of the Keys manmade wonders. This bridge is a miraculous feat of engineering and was originally constructed as part of the Overseas Railway.

You can see the original trestle work, which later served as the first overseas highway but now parallels the present day bridge which we use today. The original had to be abandoned in the early 1980s but is still open in most areas to foot and bike traffic.

THE ORIGINAL OVERSEAS RAILROAD TRESTLE WHICH PARALLELS THE SEVEN MILE BRIDGE.
PHOTO CREDIT: STACYE LEE

As you're traveling on the Seven Mile Bridge, you can look to the right and see Pigeon Key, which is on the National Register of Historical Places. It is here where workers for the Florida East Coast Railway were housed between 1908 and 1912 during the construction of Henry Flagler's Overseas Railroad that connected the Florida mainland with Key West and the other Keys. It is also here where you will find historical buildings and artifacts that pay tribute to the construction of the Overseas Highway and the 400 souls who were washed away in the Great Hurricane of 1935—most of whom were World War I veterans hired to build the bridges as part of President Roosevelt's New Deal. You can set up your tour of the island by stopping into the Pigeon Key Gift Shop on Vaca Key, which is housed in an antique railway car. Your tour includes a boat ride—which is the only way to get to Pigeon Key—plus all-day access to the grounds and the use of snorkel equipment.

A couple of miles after the end of the Seven Mile Bridge, look to your left, and you'll be passing one of the most scenic state parks to be found anywhere. This is Bahia Honda State Park right at mile marker 37, and it is reported as the best natural beach in the Florida

Keys. Besides its award-winning beaches, it offers a total of 80 campsites which can accommodate tent or RV campers in three different areas of the park. Bahia Honda also has three duplex cabins that can accommodate 6 persons each. You can enjoy biking, swimming, kayaking, snorkeling, or just relax on its beautiful beaches and enjoy the sunny view and its crystal-clear emerald waters. There is also a gift and snack shop in the park for your needs.

HISTORICAL PIGEON KEY, ACCESSIBLE NOW BY BOAT ONLY. PHOTO CREDIT: MARK LEE

The next community you come to is Big Pine Key. Watch out for the Key deer in this area as they may be seen eating on the side of the motorway or crossing the road. Be courteous, they were here first. If it's lunchtime or you need something to wet your whistle, take a right at the light onto Wilder Road and look for the No Name Pub. Hopefully you have GPS because it is not the easiest place to find, but it's well worth the search. As you drive into its gravel parking lot, it's scenic enough on the outside with its picnic tables and towering coconut palms, but on the inside, you will not believe your eyes. Step inside this bar, and you'll see nothing but wall-to-wall dollar bills. They literally cover every square inch of wall and ceiling and appear to be layers deep. The story goes that in the 70s and 80s, there was lots of illegal drug money flowing through the Keys. So much, in fact, that bar patrons started putting messages or initials on them and stapling them up for all to see. Thus, a tradition was born and continues today as done by yours truly before I left. On a recent afternoon visit, we had the handmade thin crust pizza, which was outstanding, and they serve a wide variety of beer or wine to go with your snack or meal. I definitely think the No Name Pub's motto applies, "a great place if you can find it." Be sure to check their address on the website and use your GPS. It is without a doubt a hidden treasure in Big Pine Key.

THE NO NAME PUB, HARD TO FIND BUT WELL WORTH THE SEARCH. KIND OF LIKE LOOKING FOR A LOST SHAKER OF SALT? PHOTO CREDIT: MARK LEE

About ten miles down the road, you'll pass through Ramrod Key. We're really closing in on our destination of Key West as it is only 27 miles away. Look to your right when passing through Ramrod Key and you'll see the tropical bar and restaurant known as the Boondocks Grille and Draft house. You can't miss it because it is the biggest thatched structure I've ever seen in the Keys. My good friend Howard Livingston and his Mile Marker 24 Band play here often so be sure and catch their show if they're performing when you're in the area. The Boondocks is a full-service bar and grille and has happy hour weeknights from 4:00 to 6:00 pm and nightly entertainment. They even have a miniature golf course.

With a little more than 26 miles to go, you've almost made it to the Conch Republic so be sure to have your passports ready. Just before you reach Key West, you ride past Key West Naval Air Station on Boca Chica Key. It is in this area that you may see Navy jet fighters taking off or landing and practicing their maneuvers. We were highly entertained one afternoon sitting on the waterfront at Boyd's Campground as this seems to be right in the flight pattern of the F18 Super Hornets that were coming in for a landing.

Finally on Stock Island, you reach the location of one of my favorite waterfront spots, the Hogfish Bar and Grille, and once over the Cow Key Channel Bridge, you arrive at your destination. Key West, Florida, is the end of the line, mile marker zero where you leave your watch and your cares behind because you're on island time now. Let the good times begin.

SO THIS IS WHAT YOU FIND AT THE END OF THE RAINBOW, KEY WEST.
PHOTO CREDIT: MARK LEE

PLANE

Key West International Airport is the southernmost airport in the continental United States. The first commercial flight took place here by Aeromarine Airways and was swiftly followed by Pan American on January 6, 1928. Pan Am had its start as a small passenger and mail service to Havana, Cuba before it grew to be the largest airline in the US at one time. It had its beginnings in Key West in the building that is occupied by Kelly's Caribbean Bar Grill and Brewery at 301 Whitehead Street.

Today, Key West is served by several major airlines such as US Airways, Delta, and American Eagle. In most cases, flights are routed through Miami International Airport to pick up connecting flights for the final leg to Key West. However, there are several regional carriers with direct or charter flights to points in Florida and the Bahamas with any international flights being routed through Miami.

CRUISING

On my most recent trip to Key West, I was peering down the street to the waterfront, and I couldn't miss it. It was a large figure, massive and imposing, majestically towering above the buildings. This beautiful structure was one of Royal Caribbean's luxury cruise ships, which was docked to allow its passengers to experience the day in Old Town Key West.

It's an almost daily occurrence as you can see by looking at the calendar of cruise ships coming to town either in the local newspaper, the *Key West Citizen*, or on the city of Key West's website, which gives details about its cruise ship facilities. On any given day, you may find a number of cruise ships docked for the day. They include familiar names such as Disney, Royal Caribbean, Holland America, Celebrity, and Carnival. Key West is visited by more than 750,000 cruise ships passengers every year. They disembark at one of the three cruise ship docks to enjoy the day in Key West, soak up some of its sun and enjoy the hospitality of Duval Street and Old Town. If you are interested in seeing Key West by ship, I have a few websites below to help you find out more about cruising.

City of Key West Cruise Ship Calendar:
www.cityofkeywest-fl.gov/department/calendar.php

Carnival Cruises: www.carnival.com
Holland America: www.hollandamerica.com
Celebrity: www.celebritycruises.com
Disney: disneycruise.disney.go.com
Royal Caribbean: www.royalcaribbean.com

DISNEY CRUISE SHIP DOCKED AT MALLORY SQUARE. KEY WEST IS A POPULAR STOP ON CRUISE SHIP ITINERARIES. PHOTO CREDIT: MARK LEE

Key West Express

888-539-2628
www.seakeywestexpress.com

The Key West Express is a fast and fun way to get to Key West if you happen to be on the west coast of Florida. This ferry leaves from Ft. Myers and Marco Island and takes around three hours to make it to the Conch Republic. You can leave the driving to someone else as you board one of their high speed, state-of-the-art catamarans and skim the Gulf of Mexico all the way to Key West. Enjoy the ride in the open air on its spacious sundeck or relax and grab a drink at the bar. Each catamaran also offers a snack bar and large flat-screen televisions with satellite programming.

Their fleet is comprised of 3 vessels, the 140-foot *Atlanticat Catamaran*, 155-foot *Big Cat Catamaran*, and their flagship vessel, the 170-foot *Key West Express Catamaran*. They all maintain the best in electronics and navigational equipment. The crews are highly experienced as well as eager to serve their passengers with the utmost in service on your jaunt to the Keys. A roundtrip fare starts at $119 for adults with an 8-day advance purchase for Monday thru Thursday travel. Weekends are a low $134. Teens and kids fares are even less expensive so check their website or call for more details and reserve your space today.

THE WALKING ALARM CLOCKS OF KEY WEST, YOU'LL SEE THEM EVERYWHERE.
LEAVE YOUR WINDOWS OPEN AT NIGHT AND THEY'LL BE SURE TO WAKE YOU BEFORE DAWN.
PHOTO CREDIT: STACYE LEE

PLACES TO STAY

So it's four in the morning, the bar is closing, and you hear this, "You don't have to go home, but you can't stay here!" Let's hope you've thought ahead and have a great place lined up to stay. Surely you'll want to take a nap before you head out to the beach and spend another night on the town. Key West has a variety of properties ranging from quaint bed-and-breakfasts to waterfront resorts. In case you need some ideas, check out this list of great homes-away-from-home to choose from:

1. **Almond Tree Inn, 512 Truman Avenue, Key West, FL 33040**
   Phone: (305) 296-5415, (800) 311-4292
   Website: www.almondtreeinn.com

2. **Orchid Key Inn, 1004 Duval Street, Key West, FL 33040**
   Phone: (305)296-9915, (800) 845-8384
   Website: www.orchidkey.com

3. **Marquesa, 600 Fleming St, Key West, FL 33040**
   Phone: (305) 292-1919, (800) 869-4631
   Website: www.marquesa.com

4. **Southernmost on the Beach, 508 South Street, Key West, FL 33040**
   Phone: (305) 296-5611, (888) 449-0633
   www.southernmostresorts.com/southernmost-on-the-beach

5. **Santa Marina Suites, 1401 Simonton Street, Key West, FL 33040**
   Phone: (305) 296-5678, (866) 726-8259
   Website: www.santamariasuites.com

6. **Eden House, 1015 Fleming Street, Key West, FL 33040**
    Phone: (305) 296-6868, (800) 533-5397
    Website: www.edenhouse.com

7. **Ocean Key Resort, Zero Duval Street, Key West, FL 33040**
    Phone: (305) 296-7701, (800) 328-9815
    Website: www.oceankey.com

8. **Southern Most Hotel, 1319 Duval St, Key West, FL 33040**
    Phone: (305) 296-6577, (800) 354-4455
    Website: www.southernmostresorts.com

9. **Pier House Resort Hotel and Resort, 1 Duval St, Key West, FL 33040**
    Phone: (305) 296-4600, (800) 327-8340
    Website: www.pierhouse.com

10. **Parrot Key Hotel and Resort, 2801 N Roosevelt Blvd, Key West, FL 33040**
    Phone: (305) 809-2200, (877) 741-5868
    Website: www.parrotkeyresort.com

11. **Sunset Key Guest Cottages, A Westin Resort, 245 Front St, Key West, FL 33040**
    Phone: (305) 292-5300, (866) 837-4249
    Website: www.westinsunsetkeycottages.com

12. **Best Western Hibiscus, 1313 Simonton Street, Key West, FL 33040**
    Phone: (305) 294-3763, (800) 972-5100

13. **Hyatt Key West Resort & Spa, 601 Front Street, Key West, FL, 33040**
    Phone: (305) 809-1234, (888) 591-1234
    Website: www.keywest.hyatt.com

14. **Cypress House Key West, 601 Caroline Street, Key West, FL 33040**

    Phone: (305) 294-6969, (800) 549-4430

    Website: www.historickeywestinns.com/the-inns/cypress-house

15. **Key Lime Inn, 725 Truman Ave, Key West, FL 33040**

    Phone: (305)294-5229, (800) 549-4430

    Website: www.historickeywestinns.com/the-inns/key-lime-inn

16. **Casa Marina, 1500 Reynolds Street, Key West, FL 33040**

    Phone: (305) 296-3535, (888)-303-5717

    Website: www.casamarinaresort.com

17. **The Reach, 1435 Simonton Street, Key West, FL 33040**

    Phone: (305) 296-5000, (888)-318-4316

    Website: www.reachresort.com

TOP TEN KEY WEST TO-DO LIST

1. PICTURE AT THE SOUTHERNMOST POINT.

**Corner of Whitehead and South Streets,
www.southernmostpointusa.com**

Erected by the city of Key West in 1983, nearly a million tourists per year have their picture taken at the Southernmost Point Buoy. Located at the corner of Whitehead and South Streets, it is considered to be the Southernmost Point in the USA. If you're feeling adventurous jump in and start swimming for Cuba. It's only 90 miles from here.

ONE OF THE MOST PHOTOGRAPHED LANDMARKS IN KEY WEST.
PHOTO CREDIT: MARK LEE

2. HEMINGWAY HOUSE.

**907 Whitehead St, (305) 294-1136,
www.hemingwayhome.com**

Found just down the street from the Southernmost Point at 907 Whitehead Street, this was the home of Ernest Hemingway in the 1930s. The home was originally constructed in 1851 by Asa Tift from Georgia who was a marine architect and salvage wrecker of the day. It was purchased and renovated by Ernest and Pauline Hemingway in 1931 and became home to them and their children. Hemingway took great pleasure during his years in Key West and spent his time writing, fishing on his boat, and drinking with his friends most afternoons at Sloppy Joe's.

THE HEMINGWAY HOME AND MUSEUM IS LOCATED AT 907 WHITAKER STREET.
PHOTO CREDIT: ANDREAS LAMECKER

3. Mel Fisher Maritime Museum.

200 Greene Street, (305)294-2633,
www.melfisher.org

If you want to know the definition of an optimist, you should see a picture of Mel Fisher in the dictionary. This larger than life man's motto was, "today's the day." Every day he and his crew would search for the treasure of the *Atocha* in the waters off the Florida Keys. The *Atocha* was a Spanish ship that sank in a hurricane in 1622, which was laden with precious metals and gemstones that had been mined from Central and South America. For 16 years, Mel Fisher and crew, including members of his family, searched unceasingly for these hidden treasures. Through pain and perseverance, he finally found his quest and this museum stands as a monument to him and his indomitable spirit.

THE MEL FISHER MARITIME MUSEUM. HERE YOU CAN LEARN ABOUT THE LARGER THAN LIFE TREASURE HUNTER AND SEE SOME OF HIS FINDS. LOOK FOR THE BIG GOLD BAR! PHOTO CREDIT: MARK LEE

4. KEY WEST ART AND HISTORICAL SOCIETY.

281 Front St, (305) 295-6616,
www.kwahs.org

The Key West Art and Historical Society maintains three sites which are the Custom House Museum, Fort East Martello, and the Lighthouse and Keeper's Quarters. The KWAHS functions to preserve the culture of the Florida Keys and exhibits artwork of all kinds that emanate from the region. They are also the caretakers of some of the personal items that belonged to Ernest Hemingway.

THE KEY WEST ART AND HISTORICAL SOCIETY MAINTAIN THREE MUSEUMS AND SERVES TO PRESERVE THE RICH HERITAGE OF THE FLORIDA KEYS. PHOTO CREDIT: MARK LEE

5. KERMIT'S KEY LIME PIES.

200 Elizabeth Street, (305) 296-0806,
www.keylimeshop.com

I think I make a pretty special Key Lime Pie but when you're in Key West, you owe it to yourself to see Kermit for all things Key Lime. Kermit has been featured on *Food Network, National Geographic,* and even Paula Deen as having the best Key Lime Pie around. He doesn't stock just pies as he offers a variety of items made with Key Lime including cookies, salsa, jelly beans, and olive oil. He even has a super website to order his wares from once you're back home and craving a taste of lime.

THE BEST KEY LIME PIE IN TOWN AND MORE CAN BE FOUND AT BOTH OF KERMIT'S LOCATIONS IN KEY WEST.
PHOTO CREDIT: MARK LEE

6. KEY WEST SHIPWRECK MUSEUM.

1 Whitehead St, (305) 292-8990,
www.keywestshipwreck.com

In the 1800s, wrecking was a major industry in Key West and the lifeblood of the community. When a shipwreck was announced in town, the race was on to work on the salvage of the crew, ship, and cargo. This museum provides a peek into the past of Key West and a vital part of its history.

LARGER THAN LIFE FIGURES DANCE OUTSIDE THE KEY WEST ART & HISTORY MUSEUM.
COURTESY OF THE KEY WEST SHIPWRECK MUSEUM.

66

7. CONCH TRAIN TOUR.

303 Front St, (305) 294-5161,
www.conchtourtrain.com

The Conch Train is a rolling tour through the streets of Key West and draws its heritage from Henry Flagler's Overseas Railroad. The Overseas Railroad was an extension of the Florida East Coast Railway and connected the Keys with the Florida mainland with daily passenger and freight train service from 1912 till 1935. The fun and informative Conch Train tour has been running since 1958 and takes in over 100 points of interest in Key West. Your friendly and knowledgeable engineer will regale you with tales of Key West, past and present.

8. DRY TORTUGAS NATIONAL PARK.

(305) 242-7700,
www.nps.gov/drto

This beautiful and remote park can be found around 70 miles to the west of Key West. It is made up of seven small islands and is accessible only by boat or seaplane. Fort Jefferson, an 1800s era fortress, still stands here surrounded by stunning crystal-clear waters. The all-inclusive tour on the *Yankee Freedom III* ferry, which runs from Key West to the Dry Tortugas, is an all-day event and includes a narrated tour of the fort, a chance to swim from the beach to the reef, and breathtaking opportunities to snorkel and witness the abundant marine life.

9. KEY WEST AQUARIUM.

**1 Whitehead St, (305) 296-2051,
www.keywestaquarium.com**

The Key West Aquarium is located on Mallory Square at 1 White-head Street. It is open year round and offers guided as well as self-guided tours. During these tours, the staff will educate you about the marine life in the tanks as well as offer chances to feed the sting-rays and sharks. One of the highlights of the exhibits is a chance to touch a live shark on the tail.

10. SUNSET CELEBRATION AT MALLORY SQUARE.

**Mallory Square, (305) 292-7700,
www.sunsetcelebration.org**

The best way to end your day in Key West is to plan on celebrating the sunset at Mallory Square. Every day of the week, two hours be-fore sunset, the masses gather to witness the setting of the sun as it gently disappears into the Gulf. An eclectic collection of artists, street performers, psychics, and food vendors provide entertain-ment as well as tasty treats. The performers include sword swallowers, fire jugglers, and even cats walking tight ropes.

KERMIT THE KEY LIME PIE EXPERT AND ME.
PHOTO CREDIT: STACYE LEE

WHAT'S HAPPENING

If you need another reason to visit Key West, you'll find a number of events and festivals happening each month of the year. I can't think of a bad time to visit Key West; of course, there may be better times than others depending upon your interests. That's why I've put together a list of events organized by month to give you a flavor of all that takes place on the island. It's a cool mixture of art, sports, food, and local culture. Cruise down the page and start planning your next adventure.

JANUARY

Key West Literary Seminar. A gathering of some of the world's top authors in an informal, intimate setting giving readers a chance to hear discussions of great literary works.
www.kwls.org

Florida Keys Seafood Festival. A fun festival of music, kid-friendly activities, and fresh seafood served by Key West's commercial fishermen and their families in a picnic atmosphere. It's held over two days at Bay View Park.
www.monroe.ifas.ufl.edu/environment/env_seafood_fest.shtml

Fort Lauderdale to Key West Race. An annual sailing race open to single and multi-hull boats 25 feet and longer starting in Fort Lauderdale and ending up in Key West with awards ceremony and celebration.
www.keywestrace.org

February

Ragnar Relay Florida Keys, Miami to Key West. Nearly 200-mile road race comprised of teams of twelve relay runners starting in Miami and jogging southward to the Southernmost Point in the USA. This race has become very popular so check the website to register early and don't miss out.
www.ragnarrelay.com/race/floridakeys

Old Island Days Art Festival. A showing of some of the finer works of art from local as well as national and international artists in an open-air show. This juried event features paintings done in oil and watercolor as well as sculptures and photography.
www.keywestartcenter.com/festival.html

March

Annual Conch Shell Blowing Contest. Free event held at Oldest House where contestants are judged on their ability to produce a sound out of a conch shell.

Conch Fest. Celebrates the heritage of the native Key West citizens known as Conchs with art, food, and music. Admission is free to Bay View Park.

Merkin Invitational Permit Tournament. Crafty fly fishermen converge to catch one of the area's toughest fish to snag on a fly, the permit. Boats launch from Key West Yacht Harbor Marina on Stock Island. For more information, visit www.marchmerkin.com.

April

Key West Fishing Tournament. Popular fishing tournament with 37 different types of fish that can be caught for potential prizes. It officially kicks off in April and ends in November.
www.keywestfishingtournament.com

Taste of Key West. More than 50 of Key West's finest restaurants come together to benefit AIDS Help on the Truman waterfront with tapas portion dishes, which can be enjoyed with a glass of wine in a collectible glass.
www.aidshelp.cc/taste.html

Conch Republic Independence Celebration. Celebration of Key West's brief secession from the United States. Festivities kick off with a celebration at the Schooner Wharf Bar. Events commemorating the Great Secession of 1982 include a drag race, parade, mock naval battle with the Coast Guard, bar crawl, and the Pirate's Ball.
www.conchrepublic.com

May

Key West Song Writers Festival. More than 100 of the best songwriters come to Key West to perform and interact in a variety of venues including a concert at Sunset Pier.
www.keywestsongwritersfestival.com.

Memorial Day in Key West. Need I say more? Memorial Day kicks off the traditional summer season with sun, sand, and beverages of your choice.

June

Mystery Writers Fest. A gathering for authors of mystery, crime, and suspense. Includes panel discussions, book signings, and time to interact with the writers, editors, and publishers.
www.mysterywriterskeywestfest.com

Swim Around Key West. Swimmers and kayakers circumnavigate the Conch Republic, a 12-mile-plus trip.
www.fkccswimaroundkeywest.com

July (my favorite month)

Mel Fisher Days. Celebrates the day that Mel Fisher and crew found the mother lode of the *Atocha* treasure including gold, silver coins, and emeralds that were lost over 300 years ago.
www.melfisher.com

Del Brown Permit Tournament. Named for one of the early innovators of permit fishing who proved you can catch this wily fish on an artificial fly.
www.delbrown.com

Hemingway Days and Look-Alike Contest. Celebration of Key West's most famous author and former resident, Ernest Hemingway, who penned many of his famous works while living here. Lots of fun, especially the look-alike contest; free to watch at Sloppy Joe's Bar.

Drambuie Key West Marlin Fishing Tournament. Go in search of the king of game fish, the marlin, during the Hemingway Days celebration.
www.keywestmarlin.com

Hemingway 5K Sunset Run & Paddleboard Race. A challenging 3-mile paddleboard race that starts at the Southernmost Beach followed by a 5K road race. Join the after party at the Southernmost Hotel.
www.keywestspecialevents.com/hemingway5k-run-paddleboard.htm

August

Key West Lobsterfest. Lobster season opens with this party on Duval Street. Free live concert and other events.
www.keywestlobsterfest.com

Key West Brewfest. Party on Labor Day at this event which features over 150 different beers. The high point is considered to be the Signature Tasting at South Beach.
www.keywestbrewfest.com

September

S.L.A.M. Celebrity Tournament. Anglers fish for a cure for cystic fibrosis in this fundraiser event.
www.redbone.org

42nd Annual Poker Run. Over 10,000 bikers start in Miami and cruise down the Keys collecting their poker hand at five different stops along the way. Prize or cash to the winner.
www.petersonsharley.com/custompage.asp?pg=pokerrun

October

SoMo Marathon & Half Marathon. Run a full or half marathon in the beauty of the Lower Keys and Key West.
www.somomarathon.com

Stone Crab Season Opening. A yearly happening in these parts; folks eagerly wait all year for mid-October and the opening of stone crab season. Only the claws are eaten and are considered to be the Keys most delicious renewable resource. After the claw is harvested, the stone crab is released back into the sea where it will regenerate new claws.

34th Annual Goombay Fest. A family-friendly event held in Bahamas Village, which showcases the island's arts and crafts, music, and food.

Fantasy Fest. This is Key West's biggest party and in the past has been known for its almost-anything-goes atmosphere where body paint has been the outfit of choice. It was started in 1979 by a group of locals trying to stimulate tourism during a time of the year when things were usually quiet. It worked because this exuberant celebration has grown every year. You'll find parties all over town during this 10-day marathon. Check the website for what is considered appropriate and leave the kids at home.
www.fantasyfest.com

Meeting of the Minds. Yearly meeting of the Parrot Heads in Buffettville. There are performances by members of Jimmy Buffett's band and the Margaritaville Street Fest on Friday from 1:00 to 5:30 pm on the 500 block of Duval Street (near Fleming Street) which is free and open to the public.
www.phip.com/motm.asp

NOVEMBER

Key West World Championship. Offshore powerboats thunder around Key West at over 100 mph culminating with the crowning of the world champion of this heart-pounding sport.
superboat.com

Key West International Latin Arts Festival. Celebrate Latin-American culture in music, dance, literature, and theater in the comfortable climate of Key West.

Thanksgiving in Key West. Dine on Thanksgiving turkey dressed in your best shorts and T-shirt. The average high temp for November is 80 degrees at Key West. Maybe not your typical scene but sounds good to me.

TWO RACE BOATS THUNDER PAST FOLLOWED BY A HELICOPTER ABOVE ON THE KEY WEST WATERFRONT. COURTESY SUPER BOAT INTERNATIONAL, PHOTO BY MARK LEE

THE 2014 WORLD CHAMPION OF THE UNLIMITED CLASS, MISS GEICO, THUNDERS PAST WITH SUNSET KEY IN THE BACKGROUND. COURTESY SUPER BOAT INTERNATIONAL, PHOTO BY MARK LEE

DECEMBER

TRIKW Triathalon. More than 500 men and women compete as they bike, swim, and run around Key West. www.trikw.com

Fort Taylor Pirate Invasion. Fort Taylor transforms into a British fort for three days as re-enactors converge for make-believe battles between pirates and the King's soldiers. www.forttaylorpyrates.com

Christmas in Key West. Enjoy a Caribbean Christmas as Key West's homes are decorated with twinkling lights and displays. Not a white Christmas.

New Year's Eve in Key West. Ring out the old and in with the new as the Conch Shell is lowered over Sloppy Joe's on lower Duval Street or check out the lowering of the "pirate wench" from the mast of a schooner in the Historic Seaport.

THE HISTORIC SAN CARLOS INSTITUTE IS A CUBAN HERITAGE CENTER FOUNDED IN 1871 BY CUBAN EXILES THAT CAME TO KEY WEST TO PLAN THE CAMPAIGN FOR CUBA'S INDEPENDENCE FROM SPAIN. PHOTO CREDIT: MARK LEE

FUN IN THE SUN

Located at the southernmost point in the US, Key West has lots of great benefits and one of my personal favorites is its year-round comfortable weather. The average high in January is 75 degrees with the average low being only ten degrees lower at 65. In the summer, the average high is only 89 due to the cooling effect of the tropical breezes.

The water is a beautiful shade of lime-green and is clear and inviting. There are many activities that can be enjoyed on or near the water such as fishing, boating, or jet skiing. You could just choose to lie on the beach and read a book with your favorite drink. You may want to rent a scooter for the day and take your own self-guided tour of Key West. In this section, you'll find a few resources and choices so you can decide what kind of activity you want to enjoy in this wonderful tropical paradise!

BEACHES

Fort Zachary Taylor. This beach is part of a 54-acre pre-civil war historical site and is often considered the best beach on Key West. The water is clear and provides the perfect setting to snorkel just off the beach and see a variety of undersea life. The park offers beach equipment such as chairs, umbrellas, and snorkel gear for rent. There is also a café which is open from 10:00 am to 5:00 pm daily and offers sandwiches, drinks, and snacks. Fort Zachary Taylor is located at the southernmost tip of Key West at 300 Truman Annex.

Smathers Beach. Smathers Beach is located on South Roosevelt Boulevard and is the largest beach on the island. It is about two miles long and is a manmade beach with restrooms and showers available. Smathers offers volleyball courts, a boat ramp, and jet ski rentals.

South Beach. A nice sandy beach at the southern end of Duval Street. A sign proclaims it as the southernmost beach in the United States. It's a favorite of the locals but a bit small. Get there early and claim a spot on this scenic shallow water beach. There is no restroom, but you will find the Southernmost Beach Café. The sign at the beach entrance quoting Tennessee Williams says it all, "I work everywhere, but I work best here."

Higg's Beach. Higg's Beach is located on the Atlantic Ocean just adjacent to the Waldorf Astoria Casa Marina Resort. It has ample free parking and is bordered by a short white picket fence. It has a nice white sandy beach, and picnic tables can be found shaded by towering coconut trees. A playground for kids can be accessed across the street.

Rest Beach. This tiny beach can be found next to the White Street Pier and is probably better suited to dog walking than lounging. Due to its perfect location facing southeast, it is a great place to watch the sunrise out of the Atlantic.

Fishing

Fish Monster Charters
700 Front Street
Key West, Florida
(305) 432-0046
www.fishmonstercharters.com

I've been catching the daily Fish Monster report from Captain Marlin Scott on my Facebook page every morning for quite some time now, and I always look forward to hearing about what's biting in and around the waters off Key West and the Lower Keys.

Fish Monster Charters operates three vessels: *Premium Time*, *Reel Deal*, and *Beavertail Flats Skiff*. They can handle deep water or flats fishing with their variety of boats. Their captain and crews are both knowledgeable and helpful to the novice or expert fisherman.

For an extra special adventure, take their overnight trip out to the Dry Tortugas. All you have to do is read some of the glowing reviews from their satisfied customers to see that Fish Monster Charters is first class.

Big Kahuna Charters
Florida Keys
(305) 304-5498
www.bigkahunacharters.net

Captain Chris Robinson is a longtime Key Wester, and you'll have to search far and wide to find a captain who is more experienced than he. Captain Chris has over 40 years experience fishing the waters of the Keys and specializes in flats fishing for permit, bonefish, tarpon, barracuda, shark, and cobia. Originally from St. Augustine, Florida, Chris moved to Key West in the 1970s and was one of the best bartenders around working at the Chart Room and later on the

Afterdeck at Louie's Backyard. He hung out with friends like the struggling singer at the time, Jimmy Buffett, and journalist Hunter S. Thompson.

After some years as a part-time bartender and fishing guide, he decided to make fishing a full-time pursuit in 2004. Chris is comfortable taking out the novice or expert angler and strives to give you "the time of your life" in the backcountry and flats of some of the most beautiful areas that you will ever see.

Southpaw Fishing
5950 Peninsular Avenue
(305) 393-2306
www.southpawfishingkeywest.com

If you sail with Captain Brad Simonds aboard the 43-foot custom-built Torres sports fisherman named the *Southpaw*, you will be getting both an award-winning and Orvis-endorsed fishing guide. He has over 30 years of fishing experience in the Florida Keys and started his career after college at the venerable Bud and Mary's in Islamorada back in the early 80s. He is dedicated to providing you with the best possible fishing experience and draws on his many skills to put you on the fish.

His vessel is one of the cleanest and newest and one of the few to offer a tuna tower. This gives him an advantage in spotting the signs and peering down into the water in pursuit of the wily game fish of the day. His boat is impeccably maintained and is equipped with the latest in electronics for navigation and safety. Try Captain Brad and the Southpaw for your next fishing trip and see what sets them apart from the rest.

Linda D Sportfishing
1801 North Roosevelt Blvd,
Key West Charter Boat Row, Dock 19 & 20,
(800) 299-9798
(305) 304-8102

To say that fishing runs in their blood is a true statement for the Wickers family who has run Linda D Sportfishing in Key West Florida for over 80 years. Indeed, Captain Billy Wickers III is the fourth generation to captain and guide these waters. His list of awards and prizes for fishing tournaments is too long to list here but check the website. Linda D Fishing is a holder of the Trip Advisor excellence award and is here to provide the best possible trip for its customers. They offer half- and full- day charters and go out for a variety of different fish. Call or email them today for information on setting up your next fishing trip in Key West.

Dream Catcher Charters Inc.
5555 College Road
(305) 292-7212
www.dreamcatchercharters.com

Dream Catcher Charters is another 2014 recipient of the Trip Advisor award of excellence. Their website describes their staff as a "team of professionals who have a common goal of showing people an amazing time on the waters of Key West on fishing, boating, sightseeing and snorkeling charters."

They proudly proclaim that their boats and fishing gear are in tip-top shape and well-maintained and all customers are treated as friends or family. Each year, their boats are either updated or sold so their crafts are always in like-new or new condition. They also have the best in fishing gear to provide you with the best with which to catch more fish. They have managed to grow every year by pioneering many of the customer service standards used by the competition today.

If you want to fish with one of the best and the innovators of Key West fishing guides, contact Dream Catchers.

OFFSHORE FISHING BOAT AT THE A & B MARINA.
PHOTO CREDIT: MARK LEE

JET SKI RENTAL

Fury Water Adventures of Key West
241 Front Street
(855) 990-0197
www.furycat.com

Fury Watersports is your one-stop-shop for all your watersports activities in Key West. They have three locations to serve you and have been in business for almost 30 years. One of the great things that they offer is a 90-minute jet ski tour of Key West. It is a 28-mile tour all on water, and you get to see the island from a different point of view. They use only the best of equipment, the Sea-Doo 3-seat jet ski which is known for giving a smooth, stable ride. Not only will you see points of interest such as Mallory Square and the Southernmost Point but also the beautiful back country and remote islands surrounding Key West. One of the highlights of the tour is the chance to stop on a sandbar, check things out, and take a swim. If you have limited boating experience, don't let that stop you as their tours can accommodate the novice or expert jet skier. Just call or go to their website to get started.

Hydrothunder of Key West
0 Duval Street
(305) 295-7525
www.hydrothunderofkeywest.com

HydroThunder has two locations in Key West and one in Islamorada to serve your jet ski and boat rental needs. You'll find that their 90-minute, 27-mile jet ski tour is easy to book because they have a tour that leaves every hour on the hour in Key West at one of their two locations starting at 9:00 in the morning with the last one leaving at 6:00 in the evening from the Ocean Key Resort. They offer a free shuttle service for your convenience that runs from 8:00 in the morning until 10:00 at night. With so many choices and impeccable service, you'll want to be sure to give them a try.

Barefoot Billy's
(305) 900-3088
www.barefootbillys.com

For over 20 years, Barefoot Billy's has been a leader in jet ski tours and recreational equipment rental in Key West. They have three beachfront locations to serve you on the island and get you out on the water to have some fun. Their world-famous jet ski tour lasts around two hours and encompasses a 28-mile circuit that winds around the island and back and forth between the Gulf of Mexico and the Atlantic Ocean. If you're the independent type and feel like riding in an unstructured environment, they also rent jet skis by the hour. Jet skis is but one of the many activities that they offer. For more info check their website and get going today.

Island Safari Tours
5016 5th Avenue (Stock Island)
(305) 879-2124
www.islandsafaritourskeywest.com

You'll find Island Safari Tours just over the Cow Channel Bridge in Stock Island, Key West's quieter neighbor to the east. Their tour guides are chosen for their knowledge and skills on the sea, and they will take you on an intriguing 2-hour, 27-mile journey around Key West. You'll have four stops on the tour to give you a chance to catch your breath or have questions answered by their expert staff. They also offer lots of other activities on the water such as parasailing, snorkeling, and kayaking. For those landlubbers, they offer scooter, bike, and electric car rentals. You'll find that their prices are reasonable and they're easy to find.

SAILING CRUISES

Schooner Western Union
201 Williams Street
(305) 290-3045
schoonerwesternunion.org/tours/

The *Schooner Western Union* is the flagship of Key West and the State of Florida. It was commissioned by Thompson Enterprises under contract of the Western Union Company to maintain communication cables that ran between Florida and Cuba. It was constructed and launched in Key West back in 1939 and remains to this day the last tall working ship that was constructed in the State of Florida. There are several different experiences available on the *Western Union*. They offer a sunset cruise, a moonlight cruise, and a stargazer cruise. Just imagine the wind in your hair as you sail around one of the most scenic places in the world, made all the more beautiful at sunset. You just can't beat a relaxing cruise on this grand sailing vessel. Contact them directly for more details.

THE WESTERN UNION IS THE FLAGSHIP OF KEY WEST AND THE STATE OF FLORIDA HAS A COLORFUL AND HISTORIC PAST. IT IS DOCKED AT THE SCHOONER WHARF BAR. PHOTO CREDIT: MARK LEE

Classic Harbor Line
22 William Street
(305) 293-7245
www.sail-keywest.com

From October to May the *Schooner America 2.0* sails the emerald waters off Key West giving its customers the time of their lives. This beautiful sailing vessel is a 105-foot replica of the original *Schooner America* that won the America's Cup in 1851. The *America 2.0* offers many different kinds of experiences but the most popular day-in and day-out is the evening sunset cruise. It is a two-hour romantic sunset trip bathed in the golden color of the setting sun reflecting off the tropical, translucent waters of Key West. You will be served a choice of complimentary champagne, wine, beer, soft drinks, or water and offered an appetizing selection of cheese, crackers, and shrimp cocktail. They also offer midday and moonlight cruises. Their special event cruises are also crowd-pleasers with festive trips such as the Wrecker's Race, the Romantic Valentine's Sunset Cruise, and the Lighted Boat Parade.

The Jolly II Rover
Elizabeth Street, Key West, FL 33040
(305) 304-2235
www.schoonerjollyrover.com

Travel back to Key West's early pirate days aboard the classic 80-foot, square-rigged, topsail schooner, *The Jolly Rover II* and have your own swashbuckling experience aboard Key West's "most photographed ship." It plies the beautiful green waters around Cayo Hueso resplendent with its signature red sails furled in the tropical winds. *The Jolly Rover II* is a Certificate of Excellence recipient from Trip Advisor and its website boasts hundreds of satisfied customers with glowing reviews. The two-hour sunset cruises are a treat for the senses with stimulations for sight and sound. The palate of color on fire with the Key West sunset serves as a brilliant backdrop as cannons fire and you get to take a turn at the ship's wheel charting your course around the island. You'll find an authentic old-world sailing experience aboard *The Jolly Rover II* and will make memories that last a lifetime.

Breezin Charters
Key West Bight Marina, Slip E-7
207 William Street
(305) 797-1561
www.breezincharters.com

Join the highly qualified and experienced Captain Dees and sail the tropical waters of Key West on his 42-foot Catalina sailboat. Captain Dees has been sailing charters for over 20 years and has been using his graceful boat *Breezin* since 2003. He is a two-time Trip Advisor Award of Excellence recipient and will give you a nautical experience to remember. You can learn the basics of sailing with Captain Dees as he offers lessons.

He also offers a four-hour and a seven-hour charter perfect for relaxing on the water and catching a little snorkeling time out on the reefs. You could choose to take a sunset cruise and watch for the green flash as the sun slowly sinks into the western ocean. If you're thinking about celebrating a special occasion, why not have that wedding, birthday, or anniversary aboard the *Breezin* with Captain Dees at the helm to create the perfect memory that you will treasure for a lifetime.

For rates and reservations, check out his website and get ready to set sail.

MORE SAILING RESOURCES

Schooner Spirit of Independence
202 William Street
(305) 849-4032
www.schoonerspiritofindependence.com

Danger Charters
Docked at the Westin Hotel Marina
Corner of Whitehead and Greene Street
(305) 304-7999
www.dangercharters.com

Catamaran Echo
611 Grinnell Street
Historic Seaport, Pier D
(305) 292-5044
www.dolphinecho.com

Tortuga Sailing Adventures
Private Yacht Charters & Overnight Getaways
7009 Shrimp Road, Key West, FL 33040
(305) 896-2477
www.tortugasailingadventures.com

SCOOTER RENTALS

Tropical Rentals
1300 Duval Street
(305) 294-8136
www.tropicalrentacar.com

Sun Shine Scooters
1910 North Roosevelt Boulevard
(305) 294-9990
www.sunshinescootersinc.com

The Moped Hospital
601 Truman Avenue
(305) 292-7679
www.mopedhospital.com

A & M Rentals
523 Truman Avenue
(305)-896-1921
www.amscooterskeywest.com

Pirate Rentals
401 Southard Street
877-PIRATE-6 or (305) 295-0000
www.piratescooterrentals.com

ACKNOWLEDGMENTS

What started out as a fun late summer project 12 months ago has now drawn to a close, and I have made a lot of wonderful new friends in Key West. I would like to thank Mike Croce and Roland "Snoopy" Granger at the Half Shell Raw Bar for their kind assistance. The same goes for John Vagnoni at the Green Parrot. I am certainly indebted to my friends David Sloan of Key West Ghost Hunt and Chris Shultz at the Porch. They are first-class professionals, and I could not have done this without them. After reading all of their books a few years ago, who knew that I would be writing a book of my own about Key West.

I would also like to thank Roderick Cox of Superboat International for all his help. A shout-out to Kim Knight of Irish Kevin's, who at the busiest time of the year for her, St. Patrick's Day, took time to talk to me and gave me some great info. I appreciate the call from Laurie G. of HK Management; although I didn't find the holy grail for Parrotheads, I did get some good info and direction. Thanks goes out to the staff at Fat Tuesday, the Chart Room Bar, Key West Bar Tours, World Wide Sportsman, and the others who have shown me so much kindness as I gathered material about one of my favorite places in the world.

Last, but surely not least, is my family. They have humored me and listened to me talk about moving to Key West or some other island in the Florida Keys every day of the year when the low temp outside is under 60. My wife and kids know that if they're riding anywhere with me, it's going to be Margaritaville playing on the XM radio. And don't kid about heading south, because I'm like Delta...I'm ready when you are. Thanks for all your support and love.

ONE LAST PIECE OF ADVICE:

When in Key West, ride a scooter. Parking a car, or in my case a Suburban, is impossible. There are tons of spots to pull up at the sidewalk or in front of businesses just for scooters and there are many places to rent them by the hour or day at a reasonable price. You can thank me later.

THIS WYLAND MURAL GRACES THE WALL OF A BUILDING WHICH IS PLANNED TO BE THE SITE OF A BREWERY ON THE KEY WEST WATERFRONT. PHOTO CREDIT: MARK LEE

Made in the USA
San Bernardino, CA
15 May 2016